Shadow Mountain

影山

Shadow Mountain
影山

❀ poems ❀

Claire Kageyama-Ramakrishnan

Four Way Books
Tribeca / New York City

Distributed by
University Press of New England
Hanover and London

Editorial Office
Four Way Books
POB 535, Village Station
New York, NY 10014
www.fourwaybooks.com

Library of Congress Cataloging-in-Publication Data
    Kageyama-Ramakrishnan, Claire.
    Shadow mountain : poems / Claire Kageyama-Ramakrishnan.
        p. cm.
    ISBN-13: 978-1-884800-84-9 (pbk. : alk. paper)
    ISBN-10: 1-884800-84-X (pbk. : alk. paper)
    I. Title.
    PS3611.A345S53 2008
    811'.6--dc22

                                    2007037693

This book is manufactured in the United States of America
and printed on acid-free paper.

Four Way Books is a not-for-profit literary press. We are grateful for the
assistance we receive from individual donors, public arts agencies,
and private foundations.

This publication is made possible with public funds from
the National Endowment for the Arts and from the
New York State Council on the Arts, a state agency.

Distributed by University Press of New England
One Court Street, Lebanon, NH 03766

Funding for this book was provided in part by a generous donation in
memory of John J. Wilson.

[clmp]
We are a proud member of the Council of Literary Magazines and Presses.

for my father and family

for Rajesh, all my love

Contents

III

IV

If anything made that country habitable it was the mountains themselves, purple when the sun dropped and so sharply etched in the morning light the granite dazzled almost more than the bright snow lacing it.

—Jeanne Wakatsuki Houston and James D. Houston

Fallout of the West, 1951

At night the pilots
    armed the air
    with experiments,

dropped barrels of
    uranium,
    plutonium,

spread sickness,
    like seeds showering
    the garlic fields

lined with marigolds
    to ward off insects.
    Nothing repelled

their flight. The children
    birthed without limbs,
    heat radiating

a fallout of waste
    in the atmosphere
    above the bay.

Cancer rooted deep
    in the almond trees—
    inched through ribbons

and coils, strands of
    each child's DNA
    that could stretch beyond

the reservation,
    beyond the mountains,
    and the next state.

I

Emergency Caesarian, 1967

That month, when her smoky carriage
    cradled you, you tried to swim out
to the blood on the mattress.

    The surgeon who saved you took one
of his knives and sliced a 'C' in
    her flesh. His gloved hands, soaked with

Betadine, lifted your blue body out,
    away from her cigarette.

Butterwort

Your name lacks eloquence.

Maybe that's why
you, half-human flower,
lure that bee: even the wasp smells
your perfume-like fungus.

Jealous of you,
wisteria climbs the chapel's
nautilus curves and iron bars.
Fierce shrub. Her cone of flowers

tilts with filigree:
lavender, pearl-sized petals.
Scotch broom makes you ugly.
Her slender, yellow pods,

April mop like someone's
tangled dreds.
In this cemetery garden,
a midge lands to nibble

pollen, and you,
wedged between limestone,
snap your sticky rosette
and drink its blood.

The Grandmother I Called *Mama*

She is the lady
who microwaves tea.
She is my Obaachan.

❁

The daughter willing to leave Japan.

In 1924, she sailed on the U.S.S. Jackson,
the last ship after Coolidge passed

the immigration act.
Her brother-in-law married a woman

by signing a photograph, divorced her
the day she arrived, threw her picture

in the trash and demanded a new wife.
The night World War II broke out,

her husband lost his job.
They lit a bonfire of wood and garbage,

dropped in letters and flags.

❁

At night, through my window,
she sang songs: cowpatch and
mortar saving the crab's
children, and Momotaro.

Momotaro, Momotaro is waiting
in the center of your peach.
I repeated her stories to the sky
where I learned new lessons.

I am the child she wrapped
in a kimono.
My feet in bamboo slippers.
My hair braided with chopsticks.

I wore her wedding dress
on Halloween.
She said I was third born,
the last child to taste her rice candy.

❀

As wife and mother.

    She moved to Medicine Bow, Wyoming.
        Combed lice from her children's hair.

Shampooed them with kerosene.
    Boiled bathwater on the gas stove.

    Collected cigarette wrappers.
        Mailed the foil to Japan.

Relatives melted those bundles into weapons.

❀

Her wish.

    During the fifties she moved to L.A.,
        spent her days mixing chocolate and butter

in a kitchen of cockroaches.
    Once in a car, between Olympic and Sawtelle,

    she tried to jump out the passenger window.
        Her husband held her back

as she cried, *I want to die.*

❀

Her gift.

    She sewed me a black dress
        with a peplum skirt.

I want you to wear this to my funeral.

    She handed me pearls
        she had been saving for nineteen years,

revealed her three names:
    Bad Bear, Diamonds and Crane.

Mine: *Behind in the shade of a mountain.*

❀

She is the lady
who microwaves tea.
She is my Obaachan.

In Wyoming

my grandmother's arms
spin like an autumn
wheel. She juggles some
green-gold kumquats while
she waits to fry fish.

Rose rinses spiders
from Silurian
vertebrae and dusts
a flint spear she found
near the railroad tracks.

My great-grandfather
is naked beneath
his towel as he
runs after Tom with
an ax and bottle

of homemade rice wine.
The family rooster
cackles by the black
stove. It pecks the back
of my mother's socks,

and pustulant knees.
My grandfather steps
in with another
bootful of Rainbows.
He takes the ax from

his father and grabs
the rooster by its
neck, hikes the hill for
his youngest daughter,
and hacks off its head.

The Denver Lady

I remember the Denver Lady well.
She sewed me
a cushion out of terry cloth
and autumn-colored yarn.

I remember her hair—
Damascus-steel bun,
her beauty
beneath her cage of bones.

I remember a blue spot on
her face, her wrinkled cheeks smoothed
when she smiled her
ginger-stained teeth.

She sang to me one night,
Go ne ne, go ne ne.
When she turned senile,
she still had lids,

lavender like mother-of-pearl.
The Denver Lady
is the woman standing
in the middle of Sawtelle

clutching a twisted maple stick,
a purple chrysanthemum
tucked in the waist
of her butterfly kimono.

She doesn't remember
the child I was.
She doesn't know
the woman I've become.

The Moon and Kaguya

It's September 15, 1989.
I'm twenty years old.
My name is Kaguya.

I speak to a flamingo wall.
Autumn lilies smile
in their sleep.
The sky listens.
A wise wind
blows my voice

into the dying apricots.
My hair is dark
as sumi ink.
I let it grow
and trail the back
of my kimono.

Now I change
into a mother dove.
I gather three-hundred twigs
to cup my eggs.
There's a blue jay
on the wire.

I think I'll go
and become a butterfly.
I weave myself
a sugar cocoon
and sleep all year.
A child has licked

my wings.
I can't fly. I'll hide
in a granite pagoda.
The Velveeta moon rises.
A mother opossum is dead.
She lies on the cornstarch hill

curled like a croissant.
Blackbirds have ripped
her belly apart.
Her cubs wait
on the powder trail.
Flies and ants

carry her body in pieces.
They leave behind
her chocolate fur.
I pause
where crows form doves
on the plum horizon.

The oily sea is full
of seaweed lizards.
The sky is empty.
I'm grey as a square
in Escher's drawing.
Yesterday,

you dressed like a yellowtail tuna.
(Kaguya, there isn't such a thing.)
Be quiet moon, I just created it.
(You're only a woman, Kaguya.)

I'm a woman god.
Go away moon—get out of my poem.

(Who will be the moon if I leave?)
I'll make myself the moon.
I rise a new mother.
My children are the platinum stars.
I feed them corn pebbles.
They ask me my name.

I tell them, *I am the pickled moon of November.*
Do not be afraid. The terrible moon
has gone away.

The sun is shining over Europe.
Tonight, I must rise in the East.
I help the wind grind shriveled
sardines into the soil.
We pull back our hair
like dried mushroom stems,

take scissors, cut it off,
until there's nothing left
but a stump of azaleas.

Amber Falls

        I remember times I wanted you to die—
when you hit Mama
with your slippers, threw

        fish knives at our brother,
    locked yourself in the bathroom
and swallowed pills.

        Sister, I'll call you sister
    because I never liked your real name.

    ❀

Where are you taking me?

    Venice.

What for?

    Coffee and books.
        The Novel Café
            is open until 2 a.m.

Inside, we talk over
    ice cubes and espresso.
        I sip lemon water again.

You nibble
    the last crumb pebble
        from a strawberry biscuit.

Downstairs, you flip through
    Crime and Punishment. I browse through
        Matisse and Edvard Munch.

I place the *Red Odalisque*
    next to Anne Sexton,
        The Scream near Robert Lowell.

      ✿

      At home, you warm
    your flat fingernails against
a cup of hot chocolate, get up,

        go to your room wearing
    an oxygen mask. I clutch
a crumpled picture

        of you, Sister, tugging my hair
    as we huddled together
on cushions, in red and blue

        kimonos. In the morning
    I grind Jamaican coffee.
You appear with braided hair

        and desert wildflowers.
    I rename the sky after you,
I name the tears of our childhood,

Amber Falls.

Herbicides Over Nha Trang and Quang Tri Province, 1964

Purple,
Green,
Pink,
Orange,
White,
Blue,
Super Orange.

Dinoxol
Trinoxol,
Bromacil,
Diquat,
Tandex,
Monuron,
Diuron,
Dalapun.

A Plane.
C-123 called
Patches.

In South Vietnam, 1991
Washington, D.C.

He panics before the Lincoln Memorial, charges
      into a group of sightseers. A 747
jolts the Potomac, and my father
   still doesn't say, *Excuse me.*
I turn to the bewildered people

and apologize for him, explain he is elsewhere,
      far from the outdoor rink.
Skaters practice axels, quadruple
   flips, triple twists. Pairs practice
death spirals, skate for miles.

He's so far away, he can't hear me say, *Let's walk*
      this way. He's so far away,
I just have to wait for him
   to return to the rink and plaque
of names at the Veterans' Memorial.

   Between Saigon and Nha Trang,
grenades miss his hospital tent.

Owens Valley, 1942

for my father and two uncles

Witness the fog and water evaporating from the forbidden creek, the vapors rising, traveling in tiers over barbed wire up to the stormclouds' layers of ionizing particles. See how the day weighs heavily over the Camp, whose inhabitants anticipate violent showers with the atmosphere's discharge of electricity, at an hour when the day's light succumbs to the dark, a darkening which deepens the cleavage of shadow between the mountains and burst volcanoes. The scene is worth photographing (if only the cameras hadn't been confiscated) for the jagged landscape pressing up against the sky, or for the aspect of horizon resembling stalagmites fitted to the white-blue stalactites of sky just before the desert's imminent, unbearable chill sets in, frosting the land and the adults, and three boys, brothers whose hair curls over their foreheads, their suspenders glittering with the latest whirl of sand—mixture of pumice, volcanic ash and glass. They peer out the doorway of the barracks, hoping they'll see the shedding, shredded skin of a lizard, the smashed rattler of the dead snake rolling with the wind hitting the drying, dying apple tree, in this place called *Home,* called *Camp,* called *Manzanar.*

Shadow Mountain

1. Gift Without Purchase

This is for the child's awed gaze,
his fear of the landscape's vast alluviums,
for the dry lids and tears no cool cloth
swabs, for the rub and chill of ground
sediments, ash and sand, allergens—
mice dandruff and droppings, this is for
his attempt to breathe air, saccular
spasms inside his impenetrable chest,
this is for nightmares inside him, phlegm
plugging airways, his feverish forehead,
for the child's inflammatory response,
(the one you can't see) inside the branches
and whorls of his psyche, for the array
of pain in his trachea and stomach,
for the inexplicable rhythm coursing
below clavicle and sternum,
auricular, ventricular tunnels,
for spirals the microscope misses,
molecules between his heart, mind,
and spirit. This is for the grown child,
the beat of defeat he never explains.

2. First Trip to Manzanar

When I stepped out of the car and stood *there*—
before the vertical and angular pillar,
smaller than the Washington Monument, white
with strokes of Japanese calligraphy,
when someone pointed and said, *Your father lived here*,
when I saw the trace of the block's rectangle,
when I stepped over the flaked remains of obsidian,
ants as large as my fingernails, when my uncle aimed
his camera at us, when my father tightened and said nothing,
when my sister dropped a Crush can inside
our temporary trash carrier—empty Cheetos bag,
when my brother said he really had *to go*
and my mother told him to wait
for the bathroom in the next town—*Independence*,
when my father reached and lit a new cigarette,
said he was through, he was ready to leave,
when I sat in the front seat with my mother
and my father drove around for one last look,
slowed to see a black Chevrolet, beat, antiqued
by a spray of bullets on the driver's side,
corrosion and rust devouring each hole,
when I eyed the mountains shadowed violet
in the distance, the rumble of thunder shook us,
turned us inward as my father drove North,
when my sister kneeled on the backseat
to wave at my brother and uncle following us,
the rain fell in big drops and the spattered insects
stayed stuck to each window, I choked on spit,
knew, without knowing how to tie my shoelaces,
the air was angry, the shadows followed us,
the spirits inside the camp weren't resting

3. Photograph of My Grandmother: Outside a Desert Chapel, After her Release from Patton State Hospital

These are the half-lit thoughts,
the flash without the coveted negatives.
Where was his mother? What did
the interrogators ask his father in Santa Fe?
A cloth spine bent with conclusions.
If thoughts privilege the consequence
of imagining, is there a limit to what we imagine,
to fallacies if we rely on the sublime?
Writing without the sublime—Is that
even possible? The luxuries of scribbles
without censorship. Uncertainties are the antithesis
of proofs. Security, a gain of the absolute.
The mark of equations: solids turned to vapor,
ice evaporating into air, moisture
rimming the lip and exterior of a glass,
chilled drink's loss of upward
bubbles. Numbers and formulas map
the liquid's properties. They cannot explain
a child's dream of petroglyphs,
the photographer's words on the back
of a photograph: *Not to be Reproduced, Ansel Adams.*
My uncle paid one dollar. His reason:
to fill one page of our album. The reprint,
record of lost hours, proof
his mother smiled, relied on prayer, a priest
to intervene. The reprint, trace
of violations before the shutter snapped.

4. Form Breaks: Late Night Apostrophe

Chilled by the sting of wind and vertigo,
he spies clouds half-shadowing the mountains
like paradise after the first biblical fall.
This is what he wonders: did the nights get this dull
in the Garden? Will his parents return as ash?
How long does the stab of one long eyelash last?
Will the pain in his eye from the stiff lash
stop? Did Adam's ears ache with vertigo?
Nothing is absolute, not even the ash
scatterings of truth ground in the mountains.
The pain is difficult to isolate this dull
night of apostrophe. His questions fall
in ripe clusters with midnight's steady fall
of diagonal rain stirring the last
words to settle the confusion and dull
the anxious spell of vertigo.
Here I write,
            Wind upturns dust. The mountain's
architecture shifts. Faultlines fill with ash.
Ground's layers can't hold. The self survives its ash.
Earth's plates break. Gravity pulls a fall—
out of snow on plush mountains.

How long did his first winter in Camp last?
Where did he play tic-tac-toe and *Go,*
learn to genuflect, steer clear of dulled
barbed wire scraps, the guards cradling their dull
arms. Wild Wind, help me gather up the ash,
the lives fraught with fear and vertigo.
Dust the photographs of the first fall

shots snapped by the camera's lens, the last
black and white stills of deserted mountains,
the snow-capped points of Sierra mountains,
spare the branches of the apple tree, dull
and gray with age. Wild Wind, blow in the last
gesture to protest the interned, their ash
black, wide eyes in photographs, the first Fall
shots to hide my father's fever and vertigo.

Write with me,

Wind upturns   dust.   The mountain's
architecture   shifts.   Faultlines fill with ash.
Ground's   layers   can't hold. The self
survives   its ash.   Earth's plates break.

Gravity spins a fall—
out of tense shifts.

Form breaks from the mountains.

Find the photograph—
the apple tree, frail
and pale with age,
the faces of disguised rage

5. Terzanelle: Manzanar Riot

This is a poem with missing details,
of ground gouging each barrack's windowpane,
sand crystals falling with powder and shale,

where silence and shame make adults insane.
This is about a midnight of searchlights,
of ground gouging each barrack's windowpane,

of syrup on rice and a cook's big fight.
This is the night of Manzanar's riot.
This is about a midnight of searchlights,

a swift moon and a voice shouting, Quiet!
where the revolving searchlight is the moon.
This is the night of Manzanar's riot,

windstorm of people, rifle powder fumes,
children wiping their eyes clean of debris,
where the revolving searchlight is the moon,

and children line still to use the latrines.
This is a poem with missing details,
children wiping their eyes clean of debris—
sand crystals falling with powder and shale.

6. One Question, Several Answers

Where did your father live?
> *House on Federal, City of Angels.*

Where did your father live?
> *Horse stall at a racetrack.*

Where did your father live?
> *Near the aqueduct, in a man-made desert.*

Where did your father live?
> *By a pear tree.*
> *With pears, ripe pears from that tree.*

Where did your father live?
> *Block 25.*

Where did your father live?
> *With thin strips of tarpaper.*
> *Pot under his straw mattress.*

Where did your father live?
> *Waiting in line to use the latrines.*
> *Waiting in line at the mess hall.*
> *Waiting for his parents.*

Where did your father live?
> *The Desert Chapel.*

Where did your father live?
> *With his brothers,*
> *transplants—Joshua trees.*

Where did your father live?
> *In his mother's heart.*

Where did your father live?
> *Barrack 12, Unit 3.*

Where did your father live?
> *With 5 strand barbs.*
> *With windstorms and bitterbrush.*
> *With years of snowmelt, glacial erasure.*

7. Death at Manzanar, 1943

Did anyone tell you
    he walked barefoot through ticks?

        He filled ground holes with marbles.
        He touched the South side fence
        when the guards weren't looking.

He heard coyotes upset the chickens,
    saw veins spread over the desert.

        He liked pears more than apples.
        His favorite color was blue.
        He liked high places.

Did anyone tell you
    he reached for an apple?

        Poison spread through his ankle.
        He never felt the bite
        or heard the rattle.

Did anyone tell you
    he loved Pleasure Park,

        the bridge over the stream?
        He kept a bird-tip arrowhead.
        He was an orphan at the Children's Village.

He thought Heaven lurked behind,
  in the shade of a mountain.

He thought he'd see

  his mother and father again.
  He thought he'd say good-bye
  to everyone in camp.

He believed Heaven a place
  without barbed wire.

8. Reasons Without Answers: Visiting the Ruins of a Japanese Internment Camp in Northern California

Someday when someone tells me reasons why
    my parents make me stand so still right here,
I'll exhale deep breaths of relief to know
    their silence in snapping these photographs
of the rock and pagoda-roofed guard house,
    where there's something my father can still see,

feel deeply for a past I cannot see,
    save a few fragments when I wonder why
they look here for the flimsy, invisible house,
    a dirt spread, a block that hasn't been here
so many years, except in photographs
    Ansel Adams took and developed; he knew

what most people didn't want to know,
    the truth they tried so hard not to see.
They burned his pamphlet of photographs,
    photos I'll find and ask my uncle why
this happened, could this happen again here?
    I'll turn the worn pages to find the house

thin walled and tar-papered, unlike the house
    I live in hearing parents say, *No,*
you can't be a Brownie or Girl Scout here,
    you can't go to Summer Camp, can't you see
these people might be bad, that's why
    you can't, as I study the photographs

38

of Manzanar, the only photograph
    I'll have of the block with my father's house
I'll copy for ten cents, wondering why
    my uncle tells me, *Never say what you know,*
and I won't ask my father what he sees
    when he relives life again here,

the volcanic ash, sage, obsidian here,
    the wind howling when they snap photographs,
my father's mounting tension when he sees
    That Shithead Roosevelt in the guard house,
a survivor's rage to let the world know
    there are reasons why, good reasons why

the words remain inside the guard house,
    parents drive here to take photographs,
their children wonder, they can't tell them why.

9. Mountain and Shadow

I don't know what happened next.

> *The bus arrived. They entered the desert.*
> *The youngest son cried for his missing parents,*
> *then stopped.*

❀

Manzanar

> *Spanish for Apple Orchard.*
> *A metonym for taking fathers and sons,*
> *place that locked grandmothers up.*

❀

In Japanese

> *"kage" means "shadow,"*

> *"yama" is "mountain."*

❀

How will you write the camp?

> *With a lowercase and capital "C."*
> *With the fear of disappointing you and them.*

＊

In a dream I am reunited
   with a view of Mount Williamson.
      My brother, sister, and I are at Manzanar.

We're on our way to Independence,
   the town after the camp.
      I am standing and waiting

at the first guard house, my hands folded,
   as if I am waiting to receive the Sacraments,
      waiting for Baptism and Communion,

waiting for the Father, the Son, and the Spirit—
   for the gift of flames or tongues.
      Before flesh parted with spirit,

our grandparents and relatives were here. . .
   Suddenly, my niece and nephew appear.
      I say our relatives' bodies aren't buried

below the cemetery marker
   with Japanese calligraphy,
      but their spirits reside here.

Whatever is left of this camp,
   my niece, my nephew,
      is your legacy.

Your grandfather lived here.
   Every year in the middle of summer,
      I stood here with your father and aunt.

III

Plums

The turtle stalls
inside its shell.

Sweet and sour
tree, your blue fruit
and blood-shot leaves
stain my childhood.

Honeysuckle nods, the hummingbird
flits pollen at bougainvillea
which hangs
supple along the white
of this wall.

I have come
to suck one sweet plum
for the first boy—
sipping juice
from the same childish straw.

He turned to kiss me, made
the plums, my body ripe.

Papa

It's *kaki* season.
    Your tree holds
a chain of persimmons.

The leaves fall
    like tears to the grass
covering our old lemon tree.

Yesterday afternoon,
    the *kaki* branches
bowed to the wind

like your favorite
    fishing pole.
Your voice echoed

between the mountains
    and cemetery,
I'm Jon Doe from Redondo.

Papa,
    Those flowers have blossomed
into ripe persimmons.

I am an Asian American woman,
    daughter of the moon.
The sun is a man.

Papa, can the sun meet the moon?
    The sun can marry the moon.
Their children are the stars,

the next generation
      to hold chopsticks and forks.
Papa,

the Dodgers didn't go
      to the World Series this year.
Mama placed a row of persimmons

on the windowsill.
      They stare like sages
as I dust her bowl of pennies.

The breakfast table wears
      the smell of your *nasubi* garden,
the one we water and harvest

without you.

Hand Gestures: After *Wave Pact*

Always on the verge but never touching
with something between to discourage her.
His tactic: to lure her with a feather,

and show her the skyline settled to orange;
to gesture his palm so she'll clasp his hand,
his fingers with so much potential to

reciprocate what they can't say in words.
His hand in hers, his hand talking to hers.
Her hand, elegant, with five shapely moons.

His hand feeling her heart beat at the wrist.
Her hand holding tight as they tread new air
and water. Couple out on their first date,

climbing air as if they were destined to
tip-toe above the salt-water's surface.

Orange Morning Poppies

Spring fleas return,
black seeds to the grass,
yard mice to your cat,

your Maine Coon.
Oh, how she looks
like a small raccoon,

gouging the plums, and then,
sniffing the tree's trunk,
the next wormhole.

And your dog jumping
for the green Frisbee
heads for the compost

of mocha grounds,
star fruit skins,
dried pluots   *Here,*

everything thrives
except you.
Everything thrives,

ripens to wither
to reseed,
like the poppies

you planted   *here,*
red as   *hemoglobin*
red as   *your tulips*

as your own lips,
I wanted to kiss them
one more time   *and*

say, *For you, Love—*
this crêpe de chine
cloth, for you—

After Receiving a Lavender Bouquet From You

One whiff and the smell of lavender sends me traveling,
  to childhood, the house
    I grew up in, to the deep
      dish in the bathroom.

My mother's favorite scent—*Yardley's Lavender*,
  egg-shaped oval
    on the counter.
      Her favorite bath bar,

like lavender, sends me to that one Croatian place—
  Hvar, the lavender island.
    Hold the bar and smell.
      The scent takes us

to another realm, where we are together
  in your Croatia, your
    grandfather's columns,
      his sculpted marble carvings

supporting the mansion, above chalky cliffs, coffee shops
  that serve ground hazelnut
    ice coffee or frappe,
      glass of Italian soda,

or something soothing, like steaming cappuccino,
  before entering Ivan's house,
    past the old ruins
      of Emperor Diocletian's

summer palace in the city of Spalatto, now called Split.
    You say your father was born there,
        played inside the rooms,
            Ivan's marble house—

Ivan's chilled sculpture, tall figures whose faces spelled anger
    and arrogance, eyes that looked
        more like Ivan than
            Tvrtko—his hardheaded son,

their furrowed brows angled over the lids. You say that E.
    left you there, in Split, Bella ran out,
        as if she had seen a poltergeist,
            past sprinklers and the hands

splashing in the water's makeshift playground,
    Split's patterns—splayed shadows,
        where you point out the fig trees,
            say they're the same ones,

the offspring figs Tvrtko ate and tossed
    in the sea, wrote about in his poems,
        his brief memoir. You tell me
            you wrote through him,

wrote his voice into a novel. It's then I want to tell you
    I love figs, dried and ground figs,
        this light lavender bouquet
            from Croatia, your Croatia.

Surreal Optics: After Seeing *Dante's Egg*

Bloomed hibiscus, her egg waits sunny-side
up. Her corolla unfolds red petals,
a skirt of sheared cloth, pulled and stitched with hem.

The seam's pressed with elaborate wrinkles.
Some shallow lobes quiver, her lips long for
the touch of the tendril wavering above.

Blanket of white and soft yolk covers her,
the cut for an apron to cloak private
parts, shield her bloomed hibiscus, her yellow

stamen of anthers and firm filaments.
The wind's tipped stigma still doesn't protrude
to penetrate her yolk's fragility.

The bloom can't elude how the tendril eyes
her darkest well, enveloping the egg's
smoothed center. Air urges him to suck her

voluptuous nest, cradled and waiting.
The air tells him his heart, his spade, his limbs
should linger above her, streaming music

like a master playing a violin.
The instrument's bow sliding with resin.
Mah Jong tiles floating in the background.

Air chiming, *He's Fall. She's Spring and Summer.*
The character's oval, red, for *East Wind.*
The plants lean in the way two people kiss.

Words say, *Such sensuality persists.*
For plants, such sensuality exists.

Song Played for You

I dream you with coffee, one eye sunned
    with cataracts, eyes glancing here and there,
        spotting something new in Ivan's art,
    the quizzical mixture of high art
        and your girls' playthings—stacks of games

and puzzles, brightly colored drawings
    of sunflowers, tiny figures from
        Happy Meals, piano both girls
    play. Things you love: Vivaldi, Talking
        Heads, dark beer, photos—them hugging you,

boat in Croatia, day you toured
    islands of marble and lavender,
        lavender that calms a cat's nerves, your
    emptied heart. What fills you—your daughters'
        shimmer of glitter and nailpolish.

I dream I can see your *touch*—you,
    sitting in your sunroom, the windows
        pouring in lots of sunlight, tangled
    wildflowers lingering in your
        favorite room, Ivy's and Bella's

desks, mini-office they share with you.
    The hot tub, a bin for dust bunnies.
        Your den—the statues—Moses pointing
    to the Promised Land, woman playing
        an imaginary flute, just her

hands, (no flute) playing you the imaginary.
    Songs play for you. Song of few

words. You sense how she'd balance
the flute if there were a flute, play you
a song when you eye things with Turkish

coffee, songs of a lone woman by
the sea. See Christ and child of chilled
marble weighing five hundred pounds or
more. The frozen victor, suffering
Job in Mahogany. A furrowed

browed self-portrait by your grandfather
Ivan, his bronze portrait of Tvrtko,
a mother and child. Ivan's drawing
of two Assyrian gods, his cold
sketch of you as a child, the one blurred

image in this dream. Tell me, is it
charcoal or ink wash? I can't see. So
much for the sublime, for Ivan's
subterfuge and tutelage. I want
to ask you about the drawing of

three nude men's heavy haulage, how they
ache to betray their sore muscles.
How these things comfort your will, calm
you—The sunroom's scent of bananas

lingering with Croatian poppies.
Woman playing her imagined
flute for you. *This song's for you.*
I played this song for you.

Marriage

Mid-winter and two trees grafting.
Wire entwined around pine sticks,

their slender and stubborn trunks.
Wire that could. . .if the trees dared

to breathe, not as two trees,
or branches with two sets of antlers

used to defend, attack, and collide,
impale and ravish.

Not as Daphne pursued by Apollo,
but two trees, blessed for sustaining.

Trunks wound round with wire.
Consensual, in the acidic air,

sprightly grasshoppers everywhere.
Vine-ripened sinews securing them,

like a suspensory ligament,
for better or worse,

in sickness and in health, one tree
to withstand each windstorm,

stratocumulous shower.
To withstand two fires.

Zagging Rivers

Tangled and angular,
glistening seaweed,
salt spray and sea foam,

you dive in from Split,
after the boat rocks,
and the wood deck swells

with sea lavender,
you come up for air,
the Adriatic

sloshing you around,
pushing you down through
tunnels of time,

children stoning   *you*
your mother slapping   *you*
the poppy seeds and   *you*

the Sava River near   *you*
Cikola River near   *you*
sorrow coursing   *through*

rivers coursing   *through*
their blood pulsing   *through*
their violent rush   *through*   *you.*

Poppy Seeds

Red poppies, red poppies,
      your favorite flower,
   a framed photograph of
one big red poppy field,

Ivan's and Tvrtko's tomb
      in the background, poppies
   red poppies everywhere,
on top of that one hill,

the poppies more sacred
      to you than lavender,
   because they comfort you,
grow in College Station,

because your grandmother,
      (your mother's mother)
   made you poppy seed cake,
after your father died.

You played with the seeds,
      the poppy seeds calmed you,
   you swallowed the seeds,
no words to comfort.

Fig Tree

Figs, figs, every other page,
   we talk about this,
      your father writing about
         the figs in Zagreb.

Figs, figs, every other page.
   I tell you about
      figs in Shakespeare, the Bible,
         We talk about Judas—

Figs, figs, big as scrotums,
   Judas hanging
      himself from a slender fig
         tree. You say it fits,

the figs, the tree, suicide
   by hanging. Ivan
      as tree with Trvtko as one
         of the tree's branches.

Trvtko's suicide, you said,
   was homicide made
      to look like suicide.
         It was Ivan's fault.

Ruins

Then I wanted to kiss your wounds, especially the one
on your neck, where once your head grew crooked, veered to the right,
and the one at the bottom of your spine, the scar marking
a slipped disc of cartilage and vertebrae, the precision

of incision made by the surgeon's scalpel. You were this tree
in need of repair, sturdy but still fragile, less agile
with matters dealing with the interior below ribs,
space where the blood pumped air through the ventricles and vessels

and I, who was neither a surgeon nor a gardener,
who couldn't gauge blood pressure, the right temperature for bulbs,
still wanted to graft your wounds, mend the injured muscle, torn,
worn nerves, the branch where your neck ached sadness in your eyes made

me want to rub them, all the ruins, even
the ones with their stain and imprint camouflaged by years.

IV

The Day After

I saw him staring at me under the neighbor's parked car,
caught the blue tag dangling from his collar, light and shadow
flickering, his tongue grooming his paw, his tail swishing
its black and beige rings, as he licked each individual
claw clean, I saw him staring at me, his eyes narrowing,
oblivious to the spider near him, his amber-eyed
persistence following me over the speed bump, concrete
courtyard littered with acorns and withering crepe myrtle.
The look in his eyes said, *Carpe Diem. Tabula Rasa.*
I don't love you, I don't love you at all. . .I don't love you—
I want to erase, silence the words, the long vowels mouthed
that night. To think of tabula rasa, starting from scratch—
What an alluring thought to start life all over again:
nine lives and no loyalties.

Sonnet

It's a light gesture to meet for coffee, a big comfort
when the will aches in the wake of fall for the last lover,
and the mind ruminates over the eve of the breakup,
the eaves of wisteria trailing down the wet white wall,
an abandoned dove at a cold nest, dandelion globes,
frail globes blown apart without a chance for a late spring wish,
flood waters rising, as if the weather knows, wind knows each
broken window of the house, the aching will breaking free,
involuntarily, of wrought embellishments, the mind's
missing evening logic, the iron splinters festering.
The question of how to remove them, like the lover's last
words, incubating in the air with the ears that felt them
wrest inside the canals, as small daggers, scraping the wax,
filling the insides with flood waters—*this absence, this lack.*

Japanese Ceramics

The startled stray hisses and spits like flames licking the day's air
inside the cylindrical heater boiling the city's cold
water, imminent flood from the faucet, a minor plosion
compared to the vast blast of this hemisphere—Niagara Falls,
or the splat ripple of a fly line tugged by the creek's current,
a pole with a history of catching consecutive rainbows
or cadmium-spotted German browns, teased to greed for the thrill
of nibbling the chilled chunk of Velveeta Cheese masking the fly's
silvery hook through the creek's sand, silt, clay, and algae; lost lines
of crickets and dragonflies tied to the ocellated eye
of the peacock's plumules, plush and luminous strands of hues,
the greens and blues known as *peacock blue,* thoughts that fill the vessel
again, as hands stir lukewarm water with blue flea shampoo for
this ugly stray hissing and spitting at arms in the shallow
depths of the worn and cracked enamel of this old porcelain
tub, baked with the craft of some ceramicist's skilled chemistry
with moisture and oven temperatures, compounds of the earth
in the glazing constituents of kaolin, quartz, and feldspar,
melting into superstratum matter, one thousand degrees
Celsius, like clay figurines and pottery the gloves dipped
in celadon and periwinkle glazes for the fiery
kiln. A small cat could be something simple, maybe, something Zen
enlightened, flawed and asymmetrical, rough without the deep
sheen of something balanced and precise, with bubbles and crackling,
crannies, fingers could dye by rubbing in black India ink;
hands recall *this* while sudsing the stray with blue shampoo bubbles
and water to scrub the pepper-spotted flea dirt, the fleas' eggs,
white and light as sieved sugar or flour, clinging to the drab
clumps of fur on this abandoned stray—*cat* no one wanted, not
even you wanted, until you blinked you could feed it, bathe this
lonely, this lost, this homely, thin-limbed and bony-ribbed stray
turning, *turning out—bright beige* with grey gums and missing teeth.

Feline Reasoning

Stray:

To roam about without fixed direction.
To wander from company, restraint,
or proper limits.

A domestic animal, a person or thing
that strays.

Occurring at random or sporadically.

＊

She had been living under the house.
She was black like Sylvester, only thinner.
                             When I brought her inside,
her boots turned white.
Once, and only once, she nipped me.
I was making her bed.
                Soon, she had kittens. She nursed them

in the bathroom, got up and gouged my lover.
Stay away, stay away from my kittens,

as if she already knew,
he would lie down.
He would *stray*, as her mate had strayed for
                        a lapse of absence,
        for *space*
            to meander.

＊

After the absence, he returned,
like the tom at the screen door.

                              The male cat howling,
I've come back. I've come.

The tom stood wide-eye, pleading with my cat

to rescind,
                    rescind.

          ❀

Reasons for keeping this feline:

It reminds me of *her,*
the last stray. It's small. It's black and white,
likes to play
                    in the room where I write.

It's two-toned, variegated
as paint,
                    plains and *petroglyphs,*

stargazers and lilies.
It's two-toned like Jersey maid cows,
Dairy Queen cows.

        The Borden trademark cow.
My mother was named after that cow
with random splotches.

The cat and I   mine the sky,   pine for planets   where Jupiter looms

the moon
                    the tangled trees
Swift angle:
                The stray stays, lives in luxury with me,
                        prefers that to crouching
                      below my landlord's
                                    Saturn.

In luxury, it gnaws my boots,
shreds my sandals, my Japanese sandals,

                              strays,

tucks itself away,
in the closet or cupboard.

It likes my lover who is allergic to it.

           ❀

I've named it after Ginger Ale,
                  after ginger,
                  some pink Japanese ginger.

I've named it, Ginger.
                For medicine.
                For heartache and pleurisy.

For *vigor* and *youth*.
                For spice.
                      Pure delight.

Dying

I'll die decades from now,
in the century Two Thousand.

Will people say,
You look terrible?

What will I look like?
A white pumpkin? A ginger pickle?

Where will I be—
in the light of a spider chandelier?

Will I recognize the usual voices?
What will contain me? The air,

clouds, possibly the moon?
Will my bones turn blue underground,

or will there be men and women
picking them out of ashes?

I think about it all the time.

Origins of an Impulse

I can't tell you how it happened, just that
it happened after wet concrete, a shade
more salmon than pink. Brown ants
hurried with the current claiming bread
crumbs. It happened after the seeds of
interest spilled through me, after the garden
unfurled its roots, I learned to tie shoelaces
and spell "sand," "glass," "sage," "tar,"
"paper," "apple," and "orchard," after
my cousin died, never aged. It happened
after my sister and I stood on the left side
of the plaque, after a dusty breeze flinging
sand in our eyes and hair blew our coarse
strands to and fro in mid-air, messing up
our parts, our usually straight hair. It happened
after the sand irritated, tickled the unbaked
spaces between our toes, our feet pressed
into the foam of our flip-flops. It happened
after my mother gave me a typewriter, sky
and light blue, some ink ribbon. I wrote
how much I loved her. It happened after
our neighbor poisoned our dogs, mailed
postcards calling us "Shits" and "Japs,"
after one dog died. I wanted to dig its body
from the ground. It happened in grade school
when classmates said I had the nose of a gorilla;
in high school, when a classmate pressed
her nose with her hand, mocked the flatness
of mine. I gave up yellow, my favorite color,
started a lifelong love of lavender, wrote of
my mother's face in my face, staring at me,
her disdain when I dyed my hair red. It happened

with the anger of an electric typewriter, a dark
screened computer during college. It happened
when I saw my mother's face in my face,
when I saw her face in my niece's face.
It happened with love, the impulse to write.

Notes

p. 25: "Herbicides Over Nha Trang and Quang Tri Province, 1964":
The colors refer to the barrels of herbicides. Dinoxol, Trinoxol, Bromacil, Diquat, Tandex, Monuron, Diuron, and Dalapun are the names of chemicals used to defoliate trees in Vietnam. *Patches* was the nickname for one of the planes that dropped herbicides in Vietnam.

p. 30: "Photograph of My Grandmother: Outside a Desert Chapel, After her Release from Patton State Hospital":
"Not to be Reproduced, Ansel Adams" was written by Adams on the back of my uncle's copy of a Manzanar photograph. Adams included the photograph with the following commentary in *Born Free and Equal*: "There are many Catholics, Protestants and Buddhists at Manzanar." My grandmother and uncle are pictured outside the church with the Catholic priest, Canadian Japanese nuns, and congregation.

p. 31: "Form Breaks: Late Night Apostrophe":
"*Go*" is a Japanese board game.

p. 33: "Terzanelle: Manzanar Riot":
The Manzanar riot occurred December 5th, 1942, almost a year after the December 7th bombing of Pearl Harbor. According to Jeanne Wakatsuki Houston, ". . .a young [Japanese] cook's arrest became the immediate and popular cause that triggered the riot," along with rumors of "a Caucasian, [charged] with stealing sugar and meat from the [Manzanar] warehouses to sell on the black market" (53). For further reading, see *Farewell to Manzanar* by Jeanne Wakatsuki Houston and James D. Houston (New York: Bantam Books, 1974).

p. 36: "Death at Manzanar, 1943":
"Children's Village" refers to the orphanage for Japanese American children at Manzanar during World War II. My uncle told me about the boy who climbed a tree and died from a rattlesnake's bite.

p. 38: "Reasons Without Answers: Visiting the Ruins. . .":
The pamphlet mentioned here is *Born Free and Equal*. In *Manzanar*, John Amor and Peter Wright write, "the words and pictures in [*Born Free and Equal*] did not convey a welcome message to much of the uneasy American public in 1944. Copies were publicly burned in protest, making *Born Free and Equal* a rare book today" (xviii). For those who are interested, the full title of the text is *Born Free and Equal: The Story of the Loyal Japanese-Americans at Manzanar Relocation Center, Inyo County, California*, (New York: U.S. Camera, 1944). In recent years, most of Adams's Manzanar photographs were republished in *Born Free and Equal: The Story of Loyal Japanese Americans, Manzanar Relocation Center, Inyo County, California*, (Bishop: Spotted Dog Press, 2002). For further reading, see *Manzanar* by John Armor and Peter Wright, (U.S.A.: Times Books, 1988).

p. 46: "Papa":
Kaki is Japanese for persimmon. *Nasubi* is Japanese for eggplant.

p. 48: "Hand Gestures: After *Wave Pact*":
Wave Pact is a painting by Brent Fogt.

p. 53: "Surreal Optics: After Seeing *Dante's Egg*":
Dante's Egg is a digital collage by Sarah Reed.

p. 68: "Feline Reasoning":
The italicized definitions of "stray" are from *Webster's New Collegiate Dictionary*.

Acknowledgments

Grateful acknowledgment is made to the first publishers of these poems, some of which appeared in slightly different form:

The Antioch Review: "Dying"

Provincetown Arts: "One Question, Several Answers"

Runes: "Reasons Without Answers: Visiting the Ruins of a Japanese Internment Camp in Northern California"

Santa Monica Review: "Plums," "Emergency Caesarian, 1967"

Unsettling America: An Anthology of Contemporary Multicultural Poetry: "Mama" (renamed "The Grandmother I Called Mama")

Zone 3: "Marriage," "Amber Falls"

"The Moon and Kaguya" and "Owens Valley, 1942" appeared in *The Weight of Addition: An Anthology of Texas Poetry*

"The Denver Lady" appeared in *Mentor and Muse: Essays from Poets to Poets*

The author would like to thank Mark Doty, Edward Hirsch, Chitra Divakaruni, Robert Phillips, Gregory Orr, Charles Wright, Rita Dove, Susan Wood, Gail Wronksy, and Denea Stewart-Shaheed, for their guidance and mentoring. Many thanks, also, to Hideo Paul Kageyama, Hiroshi Kageyama, and Akira Kageyama, for providing their insights and invaluable information. And a warm greeting and thanks to Kimiko Hahn for selecting this manuscript.

Claire Kageyama-Ramakrishnan was born in Santa Monica and raised in Los Angeles. She received her B.A. in English from Loyola Marymount University in Los Angeles, earned an M.F.A. in poetry from the University of Virginia, where she was a Henry Hoyns Fellow, and completed her M.A. in literature at the University of California at Berkeley. At the University of Houston she was a Cambor Fellow and earned a Ph.D. in literature and creative writing. She is a full-time instructor at Houston Community College, Central Campus. She lives in Houston with her husband, Raj, a scientist specializing in HIV/AIDS research at Baylor College of Medicine, and their three cats.